Wavelengths

Andrew Peters

2020

Other titles:

Natural Light, 2018

Edge of Light, 2019

To all who seek.

Infrared

Title	Page
Lost	1
Shoreline	2
Miles of Mystery	3
Edge of Now	4
Chains	5
Forests and Trees	6
Psalm	8
Communion	10
Quantum Questions	11
Insight	16
Conversing in Truth	17
Bonfire	18
Luddites	19
Pyramid	20
Waiting	22
Night of Birth	24
Nightfall	27
Way Home	29

Visible

Title	Page
Hanging Crystal	32
The Tide Comes	33
Kingdom	34
Gems	35
Choices	36
Penstemon Breeze	37
Creation	38
The Stone	39
Appreciation	40
Fathers	41
Waters	42
Newborn	43
Pelicans, Single File	44
Sunset	45
The Wall Comes Down	46
The Room	48
Sorry	49
Platonic Ideal	50

Ultraviolet

Title	Page
To the Wren	54
Wordless	56
Cancer Walk	57
Relics of Shangri-La	58
Night Pond	59
The Canyon Way	60
Fossils	62
Until	63
Against the Dying of the Light	64
Memorial Mind	65
Ode to a Stump	66
Upon Leaving Xanadu	67
A Memory	70
Birds	73
Here It Is	76
Requiem for Dreams	81
Caverna	82
Delicate Time	84

INFRARED

When we look at the ocean, we see that each wave has a beginning and an end. A wave can be compared with other waves, and we can call it more or less beautiful, higher or lower, longer lasting or less long lasting. But if we look more deeply, we see that a wave is made of water. While living the life of a wave, the wave also lives the life of water.
– Thich Nhat Hanh

The beauty of things was born before eyes and sufficient to itself; the heartbreaking beauty will remain when there is no heart to break for it.
— Robinson Jeffers

Lost

Covered by layers of dust,
lost, lost on a dirt floor,
sought in desperation
on hands and knees sweeping
under the halo of a light,
seeking, seeking …

a flash there in the dust
like the birth of a new star
in the cosmic dust spread
across the vastness of space.

And there among half-lit planets,
swept by solar winds,
at last across the dark face
light flashes to eyes finally aware.

Shoreline

Children splash in the shallows.
Small hands skim the top to spray,
or push more deeply small waves
that make them smile.
When the sun spreads sideways
over the ocean, they pick up shovels and pails,
and sandy towels, and go home,
leaving unanswered questions
to melt into the tide.

Waves wash the land, smoothing the sand
in long rushes to the beach,
repeated like lines of a ceaseless poem.
Where is the hand behind the even curls?
What power pushes more deeply,
that makes for smiles?

At the end of the beach,
a shorebird tears a piece of flesh,
then leaps into the air
as the flock moves in.
In the coming of dusk,
words melt away like sand
pulled by undercurrents.
Their meaning depends on motion.
Their understanding, on stillness.

All along the empty beach,
sand glistening in moonlight,
waves continue their smoothing
well into the deeper darkness.

Miles of Mystery

The beach glistens with moonlight,
smoothed by tidal wash.
Green turtles fresh
from thousands of miles of mystery
move through tumbling surf inland
to edges of sand in search
of a birthplace left years before.

At the end of every trail
sand flies up in the darkness
until digging is deep enough.
And when nests are full and covered over,
green turtles return to miles of mystery

deep in ocean currents,
leaving all their hope
to undig the future
and follow the sparkling moon.

Edge of Now

Peaceful, the evening breathes
when the moon rounds depths of sky,
as if in hope.

A meteor just now calls a name in the flash.
The dream is of a presence in time
suddenly home.

The rim of this sweet sadness
outlines the silver darkness
with all that is unforgettable.

Chains

Old Bob Marley's chains will haunt you,
because you know they're right there,
all the time growing longer day by day,
heavier hour by hour,

and you don't know what to do
except you do because if Scrooge could,
anyone can, just go with ghosts
and they will show you, God-wise,
how to see through other eyes,
eyes that see what you haven't,
joys you haven't, pains you haven't,
beauty you haven't, misery you haven't,
eyes of the unheard,
eyes of the lost,
eyes that have seen you
when you didn't see.

But really, you needn't fear
from fairy tales made up
by someone long ago,
so many are the tales told.

But really, the chains are real
you should know,
every self-served link of them
that keep you from knowing.

Forests and Trees

What if patterned squares of skyscraper lives
could melt like limestone in acid rain,
and formless find themselves out past
the foaming river, and out past
the railroad ties of bargain living,
where would they go?

Might they find that there are paradigms
other than comfort found
in speakeasies and fine foods
imported from someplace else
now impoverished by their wealth,
something other than daily routines?

Might they find that there is more in silence
than there ever was in alarms and sirens,
more in the hush of wind through pines
than echoes in subway whines,
more in the sun sparkling off mountain streams
than anything conjured by electronic dreams?

Oh there is excitement sure in crowded ways,
in inventions that ease and more that please.
There are insights in all one-act plays,
and in live music that conjures memories,
and oh the art that seeks to find
significance that might enrich the mind.

But any who have walked the forest deeps,
any who have scaled the mountain steeps,
any who have felt the desert heat,
any who have heard the swelling seas,
these might know just as much or more
of life that lives within the core.

Psalm

You found me in the notes
      between chords,
      in variant melodies,
like the blues waiting to be set free.

I found you in refractions of light
      between shimmering
      peaks of waves
like the spray glittering mid-leap.

We met between the aroma of bread
      hanging mid-air,
and wine pressed from season's sweet
      warming in every breath.

And you touched my bones
      in the running child
      of who I was
      as gently as wind moves hair;
like no one else
      knowing what quivers
      between the vibrant strings
      of silent prayer;

knowing the life-long message
that echoes in my heart
the way mystics know the meaning
words can never speak.

And so with you here
        in moments between moments,
        spaces between places,
in the inexpressible synthesis of senses,
        the reason for flesh manifest
        makes the possible
a sublime quantum of beauty
I cannot help but share,

where what is seen is heard,
        what is heard is tasted,
        what is tasted is felt
deeply past the soul's shore,

here with you between fresh-lit incense
        and embers of myrrh.

Communion

Last manic Monday a cold wind
frosted the windows.
A glimpse caught the corner of an eye
in a full length mirror at the end of the hall.

A shadow there waved white lilies
from the meadow in the mind,
and there were fresh roses
in a simple vase by the door.

There is no choice but to seek
new candles to light new lives
in celebration of freshly baked bread
and rich offerings of holy wine.

Quantum Questions

I

An empty cup flashes in pale street lights
crouching in answerless space.
A voice raises question after question
about offerings, always assuming
who we are.

We can't help staring knowing millennial
expectations might be other
than this red-shifted widening,
other than this sigh too deep for words,
other than endless
begging on dark corners.

Arms stretched wide point clockwise
to numbers we invent meaninglessly.
Behind vast dials a vacant stare
reflects afar in the unpolished mirror
of an empty cup.

Perhaps the voice is no beggar,
but a thief jealous of those who share
full-faced the warmth of the sun,
harmonies of voices joined,
the taste of bread and wine divided.
Perhaps, cloaked in darkness,
it only means to steal possibilities.

Shafts of newborn light show
neither beggar nor thief,
but endless, black-hole edges of space
stretching photons to waves,

and pressing waves to photons
across quantum dimensions
between event horizons.

Shafts of newborn light show a face
that is the infinite limit:
beginning with questions,
ending with questions,
sometimes gaudy, sometimes plain,
simple and complex, the necessary frame
around the work of art.

II

For so long you followed pathways
halfway to the moon,
tracing the delicate edge,
as a prism hung somewhere
in Lagrangian space
just out of reach of baying hounds
in the distance.

For so long you sought the distant eye,
for years finding only the iris
of a green lake open-faced
to the canopy of space,
or sometimes only the sparkling lens
of stars lifetimes old, beyond reach.

For years you were accustomed
to hollow echoes unimpressed,
unmoved, unanswering,
accustomed to soulless years
hanging from a promontory,
witness to passing civilizations

twinkling in city lights
spread across a wide valley,

for years, accustomed to waiting
for commandments from smoking mountains,
for years accustomed to standing
at the chasm's edge in awe
of blue-mist beauty,
breathing now and then the faint air
of distant homes and hearing
high-pitched laughter.

III

Newborn light illumines the edge
like a slow walk step by step
along an undiscovered shore,
like ripples spreading slowly
from a skipping stone
quivering across a dark pool.

From a shaded bench on the shore,
a poem aloud moves the breeze
sparkling across surfaces,
sparkling fresh on faces
gazing on a high lake.

From a cabin porch hidden in the mountains
a wind from deep in the forest
sings evergreen fragrances
that set tiny flames to quiver
giving meaning to whispered laughter.

Such entangled moments brought near
from great distances are the sighs
drunk from bottles of time
tasted fully aware.

Certain moments, exquisite
in beauty, cannot be touched:
the flash of a falling star,
quiet mists along the far horizon,
the lingering taste of flowers.

Certain moments, exquisite
in timelessness touch the core:
a song reverberating
that brings a memory back to life;
the distant light of home
approaching.

IV

A baby yawns, closed-fisted,
breathing life's innocence:
behold the sun-tipped earth
like the sparked flash
of discovered beauty to which
the only response is fearlessly,
freely total, beauty allusive
to all that is now touched and tasted,
heard, and seen in every sense complete.

Beauty moves the awe-struck, silent heart
to reach the sublime moment on earth.
Old hands, tired and open,
quiver like an unheard sigh,
telling stories of life's sense and nonsense.

In these moments, questions
entangle the heart that awaits
the conversation between evening rain
and long-parched soil.
In these moments what had seemed
impossible is made real.

Stars dance close, soft caress of rays
become the gentle twining
of interleaved lives.

V

Certain moments are more
than art or science can express.
Certain moments the precious message
comes to us as if torn
into wind-blown scraps
spiraling like doves, wings spread,
catching drafts.

Certain moments taste
the everlasting bread of life,
the never-ending wine of home.
In such moments quantum becomes word,
taking the chaotic chance
of the perceived possible
appearing as sparks
across wide, dark gaps.

The quantum word
is filled with long, unforgettable
mysteries, speechless moments
of candle-flame wonder,
of wave-rushed shores,
of wind-hushed trees,
spoken whenever, wherever
the holding is deep.

Insight

Sometimes the faint form
can almost be seen
circling high and wide,
sometimes merely a reflected blur
in the surprise of eyes
suddenly grown cold and dark.
The careful, narrowing descent
carves space into rounded memories,
defined by the feathered edges
of hopes and fears.

Sometimes the faint clicks of sharp talons
can almost be heard
circling somewhere overhead.
Natural rhymes of clenched teeth,
these sounds cannot be silenced.

Listen to the moaning
summary of dreams.
Listen to the resonant bones
of poets who mimic the rhymes
of those sounds around us.

Listen for the swift sound
of feathers whispering your name.

Ruffled feathers, harsh claws,
listen.

Conversing in Truth

Sitting or standing a certain way,
holding a glass in a certain pose,
some only listen to the other voice,
and grow restless.
Some only hear their own minds
incessantly and complain
of hearing no answer.

Some are only aware of surroundings,
pictures, furniture, what is worn,
what they look like.
They understand nothing of what's been said.
Listening to the whir of the fan,
watching the breeze affects faces,
listening to a dog bark,
they recall nothing.

Others, intent upon words uttered,
how they are uttered,
what language, what mood,
what style or structure,
select one word and are lost in thought
for a time not hearing
the conversation continue.

Bonfire

It seemed the world had forgotten.
Nothing moved in cold darkness
but a diligent few working
twig by branch in the silent night.

Fire comes to the lifeless pile.
From a small start there is light
spreading warmth and movement.
Those who see it gather,
speaking words that were lifeless
as broken limbs in minds,
but now burn, igniting
the ring of faces, smiling
in the warm joy leaping
in gathered hearts.

This flame might consume the world!

Those who come later cast on logs
and flames grow higher,
sending out a crackling
heard across fields sending
great showers of sparks higher,
caught by wind.

Comes the time torches are taken up
along the path now lighted homeward.

Luddites

They stand in fresh-plowed fields,
shaking red fists at the line
of machines on the horizon.

By day, they work as always,
but by night, gather to plan
and carry out subversions,
violence justified to save
what is human.

They cannot hear the decades laughing,
but stare, the change they fear
reflecting as anger in their eyes.

Blood on their hands
runs from a deeper spilling:
nothing will ever be the same.
Nothing remains the same.

Now fists clenched around massive motors
ignore the turning of the wheel,
and in the whir there is neither
past nor future:
day by day, night by night,
moment by moment,

but there is learning,
just as the snickering decades will learn:

there is no individual survival.

Pyramid

The cold stone has changed little
since hands wrestled it here,
breathless millennia past.
Fear stacked ton upon ton
high on this mountain side,
seeking permanence.

The sun warms the face,
changelessly moving with shadows
running the valley's course.
There and there, thin streams of smoke
lift life stories up dissolving
columns, spreading like gyres
into ever-widening space.

Little wonder these stones are here,
perhaps not from fear at all,
but for the view seeing life down there
going on and on, while centurion slabs
stand close to all that is timeless.

Presence can be smelled far from the fire.

Did those who brought these cold stones,
see human moments shimmer from the valley
like heated air rising above a flame?

Did they come here from mystery,
for moments that are lifetimes,
and lifetimes that are moments?

In the quivering horizon
did they see time and energy
being woven into one fabric?

Down in valley life,
In the midst of the burning present,
there on the valley floor,
human eyes see, not knowing.
Minds understand past not sensing.
Souls comprehend futures in belief.

From here, leaning on cold stone,
the weave of baskets and blankets
blowing in the colorful wind
are the quantum patterns of being.

Waiting

Each lonely, throbbing second,
Waiting.
"Doctors are very busy these days,
and Thursdays are one
of their well-deserved days-off."
Waiting.
"Nurse is here to change the bed,
want a bath?"
Ever present pain somewhere muffled
by numb vacancy
and sheets of endless dreams;
Waiting.
Shallow discourses pretend
last-minute importance,
for this is the valueless part of life,
though the most important time.
Waiting.
Is it time?
"Where is the doctor?"
"Time for lunch!"
"Where are the results?"
"Oh, plenty of time."
Time for what?

Slowly the misty mask lifts;
jerked into the pain, again,
the dream being lived slips away.
Waiting.
"What do you want?"
"It's time. Time for another shot!"
Seconds are days
lingering too long,
laughing at shaky, senseless gibberish.
Waiting.
Waiting.

Soap-opera nurses casually
sink into ashtray seats
and smooth cups of coffee, who said what,
and multiple tragedies of multiple patients,
multiple orders, multiple procedures.
Waiting.
Calloused hands lift
sterile relief from the stainless steel plate.
Calloused eyes glance,
and calloused ears filter out pain.
I-suffer grimaces reflect only as
you're-not-the-only-one smiles.

Wait.
And what do flickering snickers
know of realities?
Mists welcome a lack of thought.
Wait.
Because throbbing loneliness
is mundane and transitory.
Wait.
Wait.
Along with empathies and sympathies,
accept what only you will ever really know:
an end to this pain,
an end to solitude.
Wait.
There is only to return,
to return to shadows
dancing beneath the fire,
or to return to shadowless
dancing beyond the fire.
Wait.
A single molecule of water
snatched by warm winds
joins drifting clouds,
easily slips into the depths
of the eternal ocean.

Night of Birth

Tyrants and despots promise nothing
but injustice and corruption,
retribution and oppression
for any who question power,
but allow a surfeit of wealth
for the wealthy and sycophants.

Pharaohs and Caesars move mountains
and build great palaces and fortresses
out of oppressed labor of thousands.
Even lesser kings like Herod the Great
ignore the cries of orphans
and sleep peacefully even when infants
perish on the blade of their necessity.

Emperors and oligarchs care nothing for the future
except their own preservation,
and conduct wars of imperialism
that corrupt all people
and destroy the essence of life itself.

Dictators and Czars know here and now,
and achieve comforts by cruelty, fear,
deception and false hopes,
and assemble symbols and stories
to make of culture a history
rewritten for their glory.

In such a world whole nations
struggle with violence and dissention,
populations of poor and afflicted.
In such a world truth is confused,
falsehoods are glorified,
and revolt is common
as new tyrants replace old.

In such a world violence will not end
until the empty hearts of tyrants collapse,
until the wealthy feel depraved from excess.
In such a world hearts turn inward,
thoughts darken and seek escape
in fantasies and any small hope.

Across that dark fabric of time
nothing breathes but potential.
In darkness the dream of life
waits in hope, fearful of predators.
In darkness hearts are cold; minds, silent,
meaning, quiescent;
hope, a shepherd's lute.

Deep in a cold night darkness is sharp
as the blade that cuts choices
from the arrow of time,
heavy as lost moments,
black as the ashes of ancient myths.

Deep in a cloudless night starlight
white as shimmering robes
announce the message
soon to shine from infant eyes,
soon to form words
that encourage the disheartened
and free the oppressed,
soon to pave the path to peace,
soon to breathe the breath of hope
that rises like a flock in migration,
thousands in fearless concert
filling the skies.

On such a night of birth
all who live in darkness
may see these stars,
may know this message
for no darkness can hide this light
from those who seek it.
No fear can bury the courage
of this faith, this living truth.

On such a night
those who have found humility arise
and speak words of life
that will not die:

peace comes when hearts open
upon compassion;
only those unafraid are free;
those who find beauty
and gratitude despite despair
live life eternal.

Nightfall

In dawn's half-light of unremembered hues,
questions appear clear, as if night
has washed away all
that yesterday left on the surface.

The sun raises blinding truth,
unseeable but for reflections
and prismatic wonders
and it feels good,
warmth for the asking,
calm in fearless moments.

Evening comes and mists descend
with the same questions still hanging
mid-air, gradually indistinct
in gathering gloom returning
the pretense of answers to darkness
from whence they came.

Darkness is but the harbor of mysteries,
home of assumed illusions,
innocent of attributed evils
and frames of terror.

It is but the gibbous field
on which plays the quantum gyres,
entropy exploding, matter collapsing
to a single point of focused dark.

And in between, we, the living,
humming the edge of now,
consume the energy of a moment,
to achieve awareness of its beauty
before silence is uttered
leaving only our residue of thought.

Way Home

It is dark and home is far away.
Hearts calloused to suffering are empty,
minds, silent, but hollow voices
echo through city canyons
and small-town main streets
off brick and concrete and steel.

The pleading of pounding music,
rough and loud in smoke-filled rooms,
grows louder with the sound
of half-full glasses clinking,
louder with the sound of feet moving.

Across the land such souls
are pressurized vessels
ready to explode at a touch.
The din of their thankless talk
is like whitened bones clattering,
clattering together in the rattling wind.

It is dark and home is far away.
With silent screams from lonely glances
long shadows disappear into the night.
In darkness long questions, answerless,
become layers of doubt and fear
hardening the autonomous shell.

In darkness all that has been lost
collapses to blind singularity,
eyes and ears searching unaware.
The question is passed eye to eye,
whether the moon will rise,
whether day will ever come.

There among echoes deep beneath surfaces
time unlived drips from stalactite roofs

unheard into caverns of sorrow.
It is dark and home is far away
across the rugged face of earth.

Yet even in darkness the migrant mind
fearless unblinds windows in the night,
like all life moving into every niche
in search of sustenance and sanctuary,
living that lives unexplained.

Across the rugged face of earth,
humility settles like morning dew,
manna for the migrant mind,
and gratitude leavens the waiting heart,
setting the phosphor of memories glimmering
like the early light of every pale dawn.

Shafts of light sweep angular paths
tilting shadows to new points of view,
and there across the rugged face of earth
the humble heart raises a sanguine flare
and eyes stirred by gratitude
awaken on the confluent sublime,
awaken on home ever present, ever alive.

Across the rugged face of earth
the air breathes long breaths of hope
soft as green sprouts, soft as the air stirred
by eyelashes as they open
on the green boughs of home,
home among rushes along the blue shore,
home among scattered outcrops of stone,
among fields and prairies waving their gold,
home wherever wings can fold,
home wherever life grows old.

VISIBLE

We are slowed down sound and light waves, a walking bundle of frequencies tuned into the cosmos. We are souls dressed up in sacred biochemical garments, and our bodies are the instruments through which our souls play their music.
                              --- Albert Einstein

Peace will come to the hearts of men when they realize their oneness with the universe. It is everywhere.
                              --- Black Elk

Hanging Crystal

Hanging in the kitchen window
the prism delights and mystifies.
Eager as children, pieces
of rainbow scatter everywhere
amid flashes which catch eyes
by surprise.

Suddenly it is seen in one flash:
one great crystal facet
through which light shines,
tracing the edge,
polishing the face.

The Tide Comes

Knowing the tide comes,
shovel and pail pile even sand
into walls and turrets,
a castle by the sea.

Knowing the tide comes,
the grainy-kneed artists at prayers
sculpt messages of hope,
parapets of truth.

Knowing the tide comes,
how is there hope in moats?
On occasion, they lean back on elbows
to observe details of sand,
balance and symmetry.

Time to time they glance at the froth
sliding closer up the shore,
and sometimes stare out past the ocean
or along the even beach
as if seeing something.

But they always return to gentle strokes
leaving parapets smooth.

Kingdom

Come, share treasures:
a large fire warms the hearth,
and comfort is scattered around
in casual, soft piles.

Come, know the pleasures
of peace within the quiet heart.
A banquet is set and we have found
reasons for gentle smiles.

Welcome, migrant,
weary of struggle and distance,
fear and despair.
Here are long, unhurried nights,
and days filled with beauty,
games to catch us smiling unaware,
music captured only by the dance.

Let us sit together
by the firelight talking,
sharing what is known of life,
what has been seen.
For of such are treasures only found
flickering in the wrinkled eyes
of friends.

Gems

Strung conscious on a string
one after the other uncounted
until the end,

diamonds and pearls slip by
one after the other interspersed
with topaz and onyx black as night
and sandstone, tourmaline,
and opaline lusters.

Now and again the jeweler
lifts the string to light,
crystal facets sparkling,
polished faces shining,
and one by one in the trained eye
each becomes the lasting
that like stars across vast

darkness connects joy
in synapses.

Choices

Smoke of the evening fire drifts starward,
like silent, formless questions
moving through the rational mind.

The stars will never answer,
wisely continuing their simple vigil,
but though their perspective
transcends fairness and fears,
it is also void of choice,
fruits of responsibilities.

If there were but seeing with those eyes,
the clarity of timeless distance,
the simplicity of Unified Fields,
sensing the intuition beyond darkness,
beyond drifting, dissipating smoke,

but at this moment, feet on the ground,
listening for new stories from the trees,
watching the glistening in gathered eyes,
I draw closer to the fire,
now glowing embers, eye-level to a child.

Smoke, increasing as from a censer,
obscures everything.

Penstemon Breeze

Like the blind passage of days,
day after day
stalks of penstemons raise up early spring
to float their flowers on the unwary breeze,
bud after bud
now swelling to bloom after bloom
now in tubal laughter.
Dozens of blossoms on each stalk
tilt back and forth in near sameness
until just there, the one
with exact geometric symmetry,
coloring of a sunset end,
and lines that reach infinity in a micron.
Unplucked it may last a day more
for the steady gaze that can't let go.
But then, like all the others
in the blind passage of days,
it will wilt, leaving only the memory
of beauty encountered
for that brief moment
that makes all of living worthwhile.

Creation

Drops appear on the pane,
converge to a long stream
running to ground.

Words gather in the mind,
converge to a long dream
running to sound.

Who are poets?
Who are lines?

From formless clouds
questions and inspirations
become liquid answers
lying around in pools.

See the smiling face among billows:
feel the overflow spill.

The Stone

A youth of an age the world is new,
an age of listening for any sound,
smelling the wind's touch,
watching all around at once,
this youth walks a country road but stops.

Among scattered rocks,
like those picked up for pockets,
some kept awhile, more let go,
there appears a special stone,
holding strength in smoothness,
memory in the sparkling roughness
of crystalized sorrows.

One finger traces whirling red streaks
to where they join the polished face.
Another presses dark, blue patches
where sky and earth meet.
It will be kept near to hear
silent hopes and fears,
tightly held in times of need.

Bright crystals, colorful lines,
it will always bring a smile,
knowing it holds ageless secrets
along the smooth edge.

Appreciation

Flowers have returned,
reminders of discovery.
Gardens and wild fields are in full bloom.
The sun pulls them up like children.

Joy lasts beyond a season.
Fresh discoveries seem endless.
Sleepless nights, long days,
hard work through the years
deserves the praise of the sun
always rising the next day.

But appreciation never matches
all the little things:
the laughter of a small, wagging head,
the toddling stagger for a hug.
The sun rejoices, but never enough.

Fathers

I hold my son.
He holds me tighter,
then wriggles for freedom
and joy at the same time.

I know how he feels,
how my father felt.

The light of the sun
wraps around wriggling shadows,
the simple meaning
of a hand curved over a day.

Waters

High lakes, glacier fed, are silent.
Well they know, but they are silent.
Of course they know, but they are silent,
shimmering when the wind speaks, but silent.

Oceans roar everything they know,
loud and overwhelming, everything they know,
unintelligible in pounding what they know,
brash in the crash of all they know.

If you would learn, listen to streams,
careful in their whisperings,
laughing with the rocks tumbling,
sparkling when the sun speaks.

Newborn

You, agape with the freedom
which is yours for the struggling,
smaller than your mother's forearm,
resting in the crook of love,
your life stretches taught
and quivering before you.

With your tiny hands, uncurl
possibilities unimagined before.
Open eyes to views of the world
never before seen.

Within each quick beat of your heart,
each murmured sigh,
you translate all we have been
into all we will be.

Pelicans, Single File

Down the beach single-file pelicans
sweep low over breakers curling
and crashing like blue memories.

In the long line of ocean song,
the unexpected smoothness,
the quiet glide of huge birds
leaves us stunned breathless.

They return for a second pass
skimming the foam on silent wings,
guided by the gentle yearning
running just beneath the surface.

Out beyond the tide forever rushing
to smooth the forgotten shore,
an uncorked bottle bobs,
now and again gently pushed by waves,
no written message inside,
only the indelible place and time
forever emptied.

Sunset

The sun sets every day.

Often there are clouds.

But sunsets do not stay:
this will never come again.

Easy to turn away, so much to do.
Others go unnoticed without effect.
But something now causes reflection,
a lingering.

Unique shades of blue and red,
particular curves in the clouds,
differences in nimbus and cirrus.

Here are reminders of other evenings,

reminders that spread
to a nearby maple tree,
the drifting breeze,
the road stretched ahead.

It is important to know
this precious moment now,
not that it is the last
before the dark.

The Wall Comes Down

This road is well-worn, travelled
many times, south and north.
Sometimes trips are with a group,
sometimes, alone; sometimes, when trees
have been leafing; or, as now,
when colors of the world are shades of rust.

Some days the road stretches straight
into a clear sky big enough
to hold all the highways
lifted to the wide, timeless blue.

Other days like today, low clouds
expose unnoticed curves
like question marks repeated
as far as can be seen.

In solitude this day even the prairie grass
curves in the ceaseless wind.
Hawks carve their own marks in the sky,
and even the oldest trees
punctuate the landscape
with bending, leafless limbs.

This road passes the graveyard
that holds parents.
Along the way watching,
clouds begin to move off
on long legs of light,
strobes across the land,
flashing here, then there over
the road. And in the new light
curves in the road are just curves,
tree-limbs, just tree-limbs.

And in the new light questions are fences
and hand-built walls lining
valleys and rolling hills,
defining plots in a world indefinable.

Listen carefully.

There is music in the wind.
Today the clouds quicken and sway
gracefully.

Today half-a-world away,
those who have waited so long
for answers climb their wall.

Today they learn the wall-dance.

The Room

Curtains drawn, dust settles
in long darkness over arms of chairs,
layered over a table,
over pieces long neglected,
everything left as it was.

Covers lay neatly smoothed
as over a corpse.
Stilled visions corked
on the table await the myth
who might bring life to the dreaming.

Through unremembered time
dimness settles to a long, still silence.
Nothing felt, nothing lost,
until the long-awaited
mystery returns.

In unremembered time at last
windows unlatch, curtains pull apart,
and a murmuring ripples
among all that was lost,

and pieces are pieces no more,
dust, brushed away in a swirling.
Heads bend together
in the uncorked circle of light.

Sorry

Parents know what to do
to teach their children how to live,
how to be civil to me and you,
how to apologize and forgive.

To say "sorry" for gentle harms
brings comfort and trust renewed
which allows for circled arms
and communities imbued.

But with age we come to know
harms too large for apologies:
those who oppress and deceive for show
or careless, bring an end to species.

These and hundreds more are done
by those whose self is interest enough,
and those believing theirs is the one
and those believing the need to be tough.

And among all those the worst of all
is potential for living that goes unlived
when precious time is left to fall
into the great unshared abyss.

No apology could make these right.
Such deeds make "sorry" a useless word
that needs alliance with more insight
to make at last the shame be heard.

So in the heart another sense
makes of "sorry" a word most just,
when sorrow demands its recompense
in depths of despair that lead nowhere.

Platonic Ideal

We, unthinking, cannot dream the billion year silence,
seeing patterns in the stars,
believing the counting of days is always up,
assuming the deep will never come for us.

We, unthinking, cannot dream the billion year silence,
filling space with all our art,
hoping creations will be enough,
assuming meaning is only ours.

We, unthinking, follow dreams of violence,
feeling power in who we are,
believing strength is in our numbers,
assuming we live beyond the dark.

We, unthinking, follow dreams of violence,
as if those dreams will be our ark,
knowing the spiral leaves us numb,
assuming its pain leads to our heart.

Such are cathode shadows
flickering in our cave,
entertaining in their terror,
vaporous in their hope.

Such are pixelated shadows
we refuse to leave,
fearing the light that blinds,
and the peace we disbelieve.

Easy we would stay,
believing flickering shadows,
loving all we've been taught to see,
never finding the blinding truth.

Easy we would stay
with troubling shadows
dancing our beautiful myths
not seeing erosion at the edge.

Easy we would stay
believing our utterances rhyme
with the very art of light
reflecting off surfaces in our minds.

Outside in the dream of billion year silence,
our planet spins light to dark,
hot to cold, season following season,
beauty alive seen or unseen.

Outside spread across billion year silence,
great clouds give birth to stars
burning in the glittering deep,
shining in search of eyes to see.

Outside spread across billion year silence
in the deep we will never know
suns come to their end
bending time into black holes.

Outside spread across billion year silence
the darkness we fear more than light
collapses, if we could but see,
pulling everything to where everything is light.

We, unthinking, cannot dream the billion year silence,
seeing patterns in the stars,
believing the counting of days is always up,
assuming the deep will never come for us.

ULTRAVIOLET

The sun shines not on us but in us. The rivers flow not past, but through us. Thrilling, tingling, vibrating every fiber and cell of the substance of our bodies, making them glide and sing. The trees wave and the flowers bloom in our bodies as well as our souls, and every bird song, wind song, and tremendous storm song of the rocks in the heart of the mountains is our song, our very own, and sings our love.

– John Muir

To the Wren

Sing me a song in parting
that I may remember
your home among the trees.

Sing me that song
wrens know so well,
the song of daybreak joy
that causes our hearts to swell.

Sing me a song in parting
that I may remember
your home among the leaves
that know the secrets of change
and hope in the cycle of seasons.

Sing me that song that announces
the limits of our domains,
a song that celebrates a new brood,
careless of the perils of living,
bursting with the hopeful mood.

Sing me a memory in parting
that I may sing your name
when I am lost and homeless
and nothing is the same.

Sing me that song
wrens always sing
when evening starts to fall,
and gloom begins to gather
and mourning doves to call.

Sing me a song in parting
that I may remember
your home among the trees.

Sing me a song in parting.
Oh sing me a song in parting.

Wordless

In languages hence as in long ages past,
there is the small space,
the single thought like a wall
covered with whispering mirrors,
whispering as if time were forgettable.
The small space refuses breathable entrance
and clings to darkness made all the darker
by shadows moving, moving
the uncatchable dream.

Is that the preferred choice?

Or might there be truths
that soar feathered and ethereal
into expanding orbitals
that sweep pulsing instants
into a plane of being,
time into matter,
motion into moment?

The simplicity of light
in all its wavelengths
is not the fabric itself,
but illumines every interstice
where gravity becomes
perceivable beauty,
the wordless instinct of joy

rising through despair
like vermilion shafts of dawn
out of night.

Cancer Walk

Life flashed before your eyes
like loud running children.
I saw it pass.

Anger would come soon, but brief;
desperation, later, also brief.
Tears came, ever-present from then on,
deeper than breath, and yet nothing,
not even sorrow like rain
running down a pane,
nothing could diminish that flash.

Through months of treatments,
we wrapped ourselves
in artificial extensions:
knowing, because-of-the-flash knowing
that that time was no different from any other:
knowing, because-of-the-flash knowing,
that the only difference was knowing,
knowing what we should have always known.

Now walking the stars down without you,
talking with you in my head,
I wonder whether people not having known you
can realize this wonder.
How might they be told what it all means?

Most seem not to know.
Otherwise, there would be no wars,
there would be no violence,
there would be no domination, no mistrust.
There would only be time for peace,
and there would only be time for beauty.

Relics of Shangri-La

At Shangri-La, washed clean in lake waters,
limestone epics resound with echoes.
Reasons go unseen by waders,
unaware of stories scattered
on the rocky shore in fossilized phrases,
deaf to ammonite soliloquies,
insensitive to echinoderm tragedies
engraved on broken granite.

At Shangri-La, washed clean by lake waters
waders splash through shallows half asleep,
heedless of loneliness in crowds,
unaware as day slides into night,
unseeing how dark waves reflect
the star-filled rush, the long line
shining from the constant moon.

Waders shuffle along unaware of choices
made into unconscious miracles,
pressed into fossilized moments.
Hands holding an ancient imprint
bring to mind hands in distant futures
holding future imprints, perusing
clues of ancient stories retold.

The reality of that moment
becomes a work of art,
secured in a limestone frame.
Timeless beauty there leads
to a walk home on a road of light.

Night Pond

Silver swans through the moon,
undulous ripples through a dark mirror:

within endless visions, curved-necked smoke
drifts from votive hopes above nameless flames
flickering with the search for life,
leaving molten wax hanging,
smoothed, mid-air.

Black edges see the curve of wings
around yolk-like moons
as reflections of prayer.

The Canyon Way

In mountains a stream cuts
a vertical course with little patience
for wandering, wielding erosion
in short swipes of time,
like the beginnings of every painful end.

But it seems, in lesser inclines
the stream takes a gentler path,
winding this way and that
in aimless contemplation.

But streams in their gatherings
from mountain paths to valley floors,
become the river road
that conspires with imperceptible

lifts of land to erode
first a bending ravine,
then the canyon wedge
then with age, the deeper gorge,
like traces on every care-worn face.

Deeper and deeper in time
the river grooves the canyon way
until the human view that was a plain
becomes for later generations
an impressive precipice.

Climbing down escarpments found,
the daring person might discern

what it means to be a stream
that roils when storms arise,
but allowed its way becomes serene.

And in the deeper drifts of time
the gorge sees less and less of day,
becomes the way of deeper shade.
And in the deeper drifts of time
the gorge becomes the cooler clime.

And in the deeper drifts of time
the daring person there will learn
the shade that covers the patient stream,
like sorrow over some lost dream,
is at last a holy moment of release.

Fossils

Invisible the wind and fleeting,
gone like the breath of truth.
Today walking near flowers,
wild or garden-bound see
more words of truth, written in colors,
and yet next week, next month
they are gone leaving seeds
to promise some future return,
if soil and sun and rain are generous.

No, the truth today springs forth,
then fades as the impression
of a sunset catches breath
then sighs into the growing dark.

But when earth cracks a smile
there, among words left,
are bones and shells formed
not millennia past, but eons
by the million. Here, then,
though not beings themselves,
in their form, like pages of poetry,
these fossils speak in detail
the lasting truth of a breath long past.

Until

A million people within the mile,
crowds of concrete fill the sky
declaring, time-unbounded,
a civilization's place.

A million people fill the space
between mirrored walls, move en masse
across plazas of time
as if each bar were a poem,
as if each store were a shrine
whose path to afterlife
were laid on neatly ordered shelves.

Where are you in whose eyes
deeper music moves,
in whose voice the forest
resounds with peace;

When are you whose touch
holds petals to stem,
whose melody becomes
infant softness?

Smiling monuments are silent.
A million people scarcely notice
the flash of headlights passing close.

And yet in chaos or stillness,
presence lives unceasing,
behind closed eyes
forever close dancing
to the dappled music of the sun.

Against the Dying of the Light
To Zoey

One day the dwindling no longer dwindles
but speeds the step on that last walk
unleashed toward the incomprehensible dark,
toward inevitable silence.

For the old dog, faithful follower
and intrepid leader at once,
step unsteadies and agility
that once amazed is now
one more memory that aches.

Her eyes betray no sorrow in her look,
that look that binds eye to eye
with strands of wordless understanding.
I will miss her world of ears
alerted to passers-by while afar.
I will miss her outsized bark
unrestrainedly running the fence.
I will miss her under the supper table
waiting, her eager leap for a treat.

I will miss this wagging life,
precious as my own,
worthy as all others.

But how will I traverse
the troubles of this world
with no companion at the heel,
and how will this be home
with no greeting at the door?

Memorial Mind

Trees hanging over the stream
that coursed the old farmstead
are still green in the memorial mind,
still answer the soft rush of water
with rustlings of leaves.

The little wooden house with wasps
that stung on the front porch
burned long ago but is forever white
in the memorial mind.

Wide-eyed youth believes the mind is evergreen,
celebrates its stories retold with decorated icons,
holiday baubles and colored lights,
defining myths remembered.

Childhood vanishes like morning mist,
gradual as growth, slow as the sun's descent,
human years sliding over the horizon.
Thus the mind is exposed as deciduous,
memories flattened, turning red and gold
when time stretches its autumnal reasons.

And as the air turns colder,
winds pull brittle reflections
from their limbs to fall away
mingling into the compost
we call culture.

Ode to a Stump

The body, it can be told,
will become the softness
of moss.

There in the glen,
all the rings of life
lose their lines to frass
that fades softer and softer
in the hollow core
into the humus of yesterday,
the peat that holds
the forest of sapling roots.

What of the mind
and all those memories
beautiful as the green sparkle
shifting in the gentle breeze,
beautiful as translucent shine
holding, holding the sun
to its covenant.

Beyond the glen, only light
unending and ever-reflecting,
only hope drifting
like the aroma of pine
whispering rustling hymns,
only love will join

all the points of light
into the eternal memory
embedded in the night.

Upon Leaving Xanadu

I

Just down from that beautiful lake
silent among glaciers, the rush
disappeared underground as remembered,
painfully.

Long and wide, the deep pool moves,
catching profusions and fusing.
A surface there open to the sky
slips over the edge, flashing.

The changing earth never looks back,
but brings circling memory
painful searching, leaving behind.
Remember rain and melting snow,
like tears gathering into pools,
soaking the wet earth, seeking
secret currents and oceans.

Onward ever onward unstoppable
seek cherished moments reflected
and the cavern beneath the crust
imitating lake before and ocean after.

Remember rain and dreams,
fear of lies, and giving anyway;
remember leaving,
empty, remember leaving.

II

Kneeling beside a clear, dark stream,
hands cupped like a pale chalice,

remember golden freedom,
green-eyed wonder,
splashing, laughing, swirling, dancing.
Here all is lost of depths but the vow
ringing through deep caves,
and ice-locked catacombs.

Hands cup the surface spring,
and rising, wander between
memories of the mountain lake
and wider visions of oceans.

Now footprints in the snow
in painful silence know
the burial may be my own.

Ache with dreams of caverns
carved to crystal hollows.
Ache for the hidden rush to surface.

Footprints made, remade,
wander onward, always disappearing,
toward forests and plains,
seeking the stream to drink again.

III

The current is strong within,
holds the soul to promises
that free the wayward spirit
to communion with skies,
bright and clear as the dream of seas,
bounded only by memories,
falling like cool rain
to the pool again.

Mountain peaks seek the plains,
lake seeks ocean.
Drink, and drink again
these precious, surface moments,
repeating long screams of seashores
celebrating all the last moments.

Drink, and drink again,
dreaming and remembering dreams.
The sacrifice sings of love.
Wander onward knowing this wide stream
leads beyond plains to oceans,
knowing the rush moves
onward in the seeking,
knowing of that moment when we
enter the ocean together.

A Memory

I

I wonder this first frost has parted us
in the slender waning of the soul,
like so many fallen leaves damp with decay.
Now it seems wandering these freezing paths,
I forget, but it is only the numbing cold.
They say our problem deals with death,
but I know it is the widening darkness
between the stars.

I realized sitting in our old haunts
and drifting over silent paths,
we were blind.
Ah, but didn't we live,
drunk with wonder,
excited with concentration,
rolling in private jokes,
mindless of reality,
mindless of the rushing sun.

Oh, what next, Destroyer,
lying to the moon whose delicate tips
like ivory fingernails tear the canopy
of darkness on the way down?
Won't even death satiate your madness?
Why do you press for this lingering insanity,
this repeating question
scraping ice-covered brains?

II

I remember we rushed with the summer sun,
waxing strong and free in bright discoveries,
blazing with anticipation and truth.

Was it the sun ate you,
or your own laughter blindly bursting
on the edges of experiences
only half known, but felt fully,
like a meteor in its fiery fall?

One evening, a wide, red autumn moon
chilled me to a dream of winter
and bare branches black
against the horizon and the pale moon.
Then I first awoke
and saw your burning body in the shade.

III

Footsteps are muffled by the closing fog
and fallen leaves, damp on the cement.
I was late but my watch stopped,
and as I walked slower, mind wandering,
I became timeless, like you,
with only frozen limbs
cracking together in the wind.

I remember the day:
all of us together because of you
celebrating something without you,
and afterwards, gathering to eat,
we reminisced, laughing,
and upstairs you were dying.

I remember the moment
returning, others gone ahead,
before the mirror, I felt your touch.
Struck solid, looking into my own eyes,
I felt my head lift.
A breath on the pane, and you were gone,
taking the world with you.

They came to me crying,
but I already knew. No one believed,
but neither did they your death.
That night was dark and silent
but for branches cracking in the slow wind.
Now I hear my arms, my legs, my fingers
cracking in the wind, ice-covered.
I envy your freedom.

IV

Someday ice-covered planets
will thaw; the moon, fall into the sea
saying follow me.
Darkness and light
will reunite in green depths,
and all will be peaceful and free.

Do I believe?
Huddled in darkness,
hearing the rhythmic cracking,
I must. And then I remember
the breath on the pane,
like mist over the moon
escaping into vapor,
and no longer feel the need
to question.

Birds

I

Just another winter for some passing
from one great distance on to another.
They gather in feathered swirls
here at the feeder to chat,
as if this arbor were meant only for them.

Unaware of hidden eyes and caring hands,
they rest and eat, ever expecting
full granaries.
To them, time is but an instinct;
distance, but an urge expressed day by day.

They do not know this winter
is like no other.
They cannot know
that when their route returns
from those warmer, distant moments,
en route to other distant moments,
there will be no grain here,
no feeder, no caring hands,
no hidden eyes, brimming with the joy
of their passing beauty,
full of appreciation
for each of their moments.

Unaware of the soon vacant house,
unaware of the journey that ends here,
they will know only that food
must be elsewhere.

From here, now near the slowing heart,
Their distances are not really far,

not nearly so far as a simple trip
through a vacant house,
not so far as the closing of a door.

II

It can be said that a night
without sleep is a lifetime,
especially that night that is the last.

Ah, Mother, tread softly
the dark web that is this night,
for though I cry as a child
I cannot go with you,
nor hold you here.

Oh, Mother, where now is home?
Cherished accumulations of a lifetime
will be apportioned,
silver and blankets there,
suncatchers and teapot here,
house sold, perhaps to one
who won't attract or even see birds.

Darkness laughs
at the grandeur of possessions,
the vanity of ownership.
What once seemed like home,
will matter only as drying paint
on a palette to the finished painting
and the absent painter.

Ah, Mother, sleep the long night
in a dream that could be home,
a sixth-sense place filled
with voices I cannot hear
to whom this night you nod
an agreement I cannot question.

III

It could be a place
where trees spread wide
their branches like wings hovering
over a nest and quiet shade waits
calmly for the flock, wing-weary,
to return home.

How little birds know.
How much birds know.

For birds the only bequest
is beauty of feather
and beauty of songs which pierce
the darkness, announcing
ever-moving, invisible boundaries,
and transitions of light,
the coming of morning,
the passing of light.

Birds sing in the moment,
perhaps grateful for what is,
perhaps hoping for what might be
in the settling of a nest.

Ah, Mother, in the end
the cherished heritage from you
is the courage of your smile,
your depth of appreciation,
and your vision of birds.

Here It Is
I

Here it is at last,
like a word once forgotten
or misunderstood,
then on the verge,
then remembered and spoken.
Here our two hands meet
the way the years of my life
fit firmly into yours,
though I'd not always seen it so.
Here it is:
all those years compressed
to a single moment,
the clasp of two hands.

II

How long has it been since this grip held
beyond symbol to a deeper meeting?
Childhood? When tagging along
my small hand would hold
secure in yours?
Now following is impossible,
yet still we hold the clasp.
Adolescence? When handshakes
came to represent the sum
of shared experience,
unspoken understanding
expressed in farewells?
Now where are symbols of life
unfolding you gave me?
Recently, when departing
the grasp held a little longer,
resetting the focus.
I never really thought
we would come to this,
the last goodbye.

III

Here it is held long,
never more clearly focused
on so much at once than now.
All the private times between us,
games and dreams,
drifting in boats on streams.
And public times, ceremonies,
details of all those years
pressed in a single moment
together between our hands
like leaves in a book.
The sun sets and we smile at the beauty
beyond all this, the fullness of life
that always exists.

City lights below begin to appear
extending away from the hospital,
somehow bringing us close
as the stars, to eternity.

IV

Here am I
like Thomas unbelieving,
holding the palm in mine,
listening to words
we try to ignore, words
describing the truth
that this life, however good, ends.
I grieve already,
sorrow for the tomorrow
you will not know.

V

Here it is,
the moment our perspectives change

to a difference I cannot comprehend,
the moment your hand slips below
cold waves.
I feel the coldness touch me,
and cling to your hand as a child
still needing security,
tightly, as tightly as I will
hold my children, and all
the moments I have left,
now I know.
I cling beyond your leaving,
beyond calling "Daddy,"
as if I could offer you security
where you are going,
as if I could comfort you beyond,
as if I could hold you here,
as if I will lose the meaning
of this, our last moment together,
as if I could set the focus
once and for all.

VI

Here it is,
the moment our hands part,
changed by the final edge
and by appreciation
for life's intensity,
the moment our hands part,
as they must if there is to be
meaning in the pain,
or freedom in seeing boundaries.

Coldness lingers:
words freeze which would tell others.
As they shatter, I lose myself.

Yet there on the phone
wordless, your words return.
Weeping stops, suddenly,
your giant hand enfolds me
in the sounds of hymns.

VII

Here am I
breathing something
which cannot die,
drawn by what I hear.
I know the pull still between us,
invisible as the force
bonding giant stars.
I know your presence.
Here am I
whose mind has turned
if eyes cannot.

VIII

I miss you here,
for it is hard not to depend
on the light we see leaving us.
Now trees are empty,
leaves, scattered, palms up.
I don't believe this empty silence,
but here it is.
I miss you in a world
where only the visible
matters. And yet,
for all you taught me,
there is something in death
you could not have taught in life:
the invisible pull always there,
beyond all boundaries.

IX

Here it is
like a cup of words
poured full over a lifetime
which I take to pass
to others, one by one.
And now my flask no longer sits
or uselessly spills,
but pours more into this cup,
mixing the fullness
someday for passing
hand to hand.

Requiem for Dreams

Where is that gentle heart
that beats the beat of youth,
searching untrod and unpeeled
for hints of eternal truths?

Where is that gentle heart
in green-eyed wonder reaching
unplanned the novel thought
for hints of future meaning?

Where is that gentle heart
that danced so freely in the rain,
heedless of distant winter
and inevitable times of pain?

Now as dreams of life begin to fade,
brittle, scattered, and wind-blown
from bare branches of memory,
the tattered heart begins to slow.

Now dreams of life decay
to compost of gratitude and hope
for generations yet to be,
nurturing roots for stories to grow.

Yet life's unchoiced dreams soak deep
into unseeable chambers of sorrow,
all of life unshared an ache of heart
for all that was lost of precious flowers.

Where is that gentle heart
that will never know reasons for pain
nor even the cleansing rain
that once was the joyous part?

Caverna

Had I waited the counting of the days
perhaps younger arms
would have saved the world,
spread peace in great white wings,
or perhaps awakened all the lost minds
with great peals of morning bells,
or perhaps restrained excess unthought
to unpollute forests and streams,

but no, I;
or would I,

would I have seen the same air rise
from mountain lakes,
sat the same ocean roar,
spoken that silent language of forest green,
breathed the breath of elk and wolf,
swept the soar of feathered hawk,
or would I have tasted limestone dust
and even licked the sparkle of quartz?

Had I waited the counting of the hours
perhaps the melody would have found
different harmonies and lost resolutions,
unhung the forgotten key
so long unchosen,
or perhaps impressionist views
would not have dried
like pastures of droughted husks,

but no, I;
or would there,

would there have been more than this
or maybe less,
or would there have been
the same shared joys,
the same shared griefs,
or would there have been raging tensors
or unangered bliss,
or even the same, the same felt hearts?

Had I waited the counting of minutes
perhaps all the lost moments
that drip crevasses in hearts,
that seep the ache in minds,
that open the cavernous soul
to dreamless sorrow,
perhaps all the lost moments
would have surfaced to dance again.

Had I waited the counting of the days
perhaps humility would have sprouted learning
that blooms in gratitude, and fruited, finds wisdom,

but no, I

Delicate Time

Delicate, silver-haired time appears
fearsome with slitted eyes and narrow teeth
to those who deny its truth.
Delicate, silver-haired time is blind
to the future, but sees clearly the past,
sees forests before the fire,
green valleys before the flood,
great cities before their abandonment,
castles before their desolation.

If you would find the hope
that escapes from sorrow
like rain from the gloom of clouds,
then listen for the stories told
by delicate, silver-haired time.
You may not learn understanding
from the ancient beauty of those myths,
but you will find strength
in the quiet meaning of those words.

And there, square in the open gray eyes
of delicate, silver-haired time,
you will sense the truth in their leisure,
peace in their endless tolerance,
faith in their fearless wonder,
beauty in their choiceless choosing.
And in the hymns sung
by delicate, silver-haired time
you will find ease to your pain,

and release to set adrift
among the sparkling stars.
And holding the trembling hands
of delicate, silver-haired time,
you will find freedom in the friendship
of the long awaited dark.

www.ingramcontent.com/pod-product-compliance
Lightning Source LLC
Chambersburg PA
CBHW071410290426
44108CB00014B/1767